STRENGTH
FOR YOUR
DAY

R. T. AND LOUISE
KENDALL

Charisma
HOUSE
A STRANG COMPANY

Most STRANG COMMUNICATIONS/CHARISMA HOUSE/SILOAM products are available at special quantity discounts for bulk purchase for sales promotions, premiums, fund-raising, and educational needs. For details, write Strang Communications/Charisma House/Siloam, 600 Rinehart Road, Lake Mary, Florida 32746, or telephone (407) 333-0600.

STRENGTH FOR YOUR DAY compiled by R. T. and Louise Kendall
Published by Charisma House
A Strang Company
600 Rinehart Road
Lake Mary, Florida 32746
www.charismahouse.com

Cover design by Lakeside Design
Interior design by Terry Clifton

Library of Congress Cataloging-in-Publication Data
Great Christian prayers.
Strength for your day / compiled by R.T. and Louise Kendall.
p. cm.
Originally published: Great Christian prayers.
Includes index.
ISBN 1-59185-804-6 (casebound)
1. Prayers. 2. Devotional calendars.   I. Kendall, R. T.
II. Kendall, Louise. III. Title.
BV245.G64 2005
242'.2--dc22
                                              2005019393

This book was previously published as *Great Christian Prayers* by Hodder & Stoughton, ISBN 0-340-75609-8, copyright © 2000.

First Edition

05 06 07 08 09 —987654321
Printed in the United States of America

CONTENTS

FOREWORD

*T*here are three stages in prayer. The first is basically "God bless me, Mommy, and Daddy," with a shopping list to a God who is there to deliver our wishes. The second is once we have come alive to the Lord Jesus as our Savior. The Holy Spirit brings us into a personal relationship, and prayer normally moves into worship, conversation, sharing, and desiring God's will, although remnants of the first sort of praying can sadly linger and confuse. The third is when we begin to hunger and thirst for God, to become like St. Paul when he longs to know Christ, the power of His resurrection, and the fellowship of His sufferings. Here prayer starts to explore the deep wonders of God in devotion and worship as well as in far more comprehensive intercession. This is where this marvelous book takes us.

When Louise Kendall talked about her exploration into the prayers of Christians across the centuries, her passion, excitement, and deepened devotion to God glowed from her heart. She had been ready to explore the prayers of saints who had different Christian affiliations and found the throb of her own heart matching theirs. Although extempore prayer is still integral to her prayer life, she discovered that in written prayers there could be gathered expressions of deep devotion, phrases with profound insight, and a range of confession, worship, and intercession that left much extempore praying in the fading shadows.

That Louise and RT have now turned that

great discovery into this book is a gift to the whole church. Not all the prayers will ring bells with us, but most will strike an inner chord and will come to be part of our own prayer life in years to come. We move over the centuries with prayers from Augustine, Corrie ten Boom, Newman, Campolo, Luther, Chaike, Lancelot Andrewes (who blew my prayer life into new orbits), and so many others. Our hearts are warmed by Timothy Dudley-Smith's beautifully poetic yet insightful prayers, with glorious phrases like "the choir of stars." I am so glad that the prayer (February 17) of the Confederate soldier just before he died in the battle of Richmond is here, as I use it frequently. Whenever I quote it everyone wants a copy…it is penetratingly moving. You will want to mark the prayers that stand out for you as you use the book across a year and then return to embrace them as part of your own devotion. It will help us all to move deeper into true prayer to our glorious Lord. For all the passion, research, and hard work that has gone into this gem of a book we are all in the debt of two very special people…Louise and R. T. Kendall.

—Rt. Rev. Dr. Michael S. Baughen
Bishop of Chester, 1982–1996
Rector of All Souls, Langham Place,
London, 1970–1982

PREFACE

On Christmas Day 1998 I gave my wife, Louise, an old copy of *Great Souls at Prayer* (1898), ancient prayers selected and arranged by Mrs. Mary W. Tileston. Some months before, Robert and Beth Amess loaned Louise their only copy, but she wanted one of her own. A few weeks before Christmas I began looking high and low in London for this book. Two days before Christmas I was given a tip that Pendlebury's, a second-hand bookshop near Seven Sisters in London, might have a copy. They did. It cost me only £3, but you would have thought I had given Louise a gold necklace when she opened that present! She wept. Having a liturgical background has given her a love for ancient prayers, and Robert and Beth's copy had formed part of her daily devotions.

You can imagine my astonishment when, out of the blue less than a month later, David Moloney of Hodder & Stoughton asked me to compile a book of prayers, which they suggested calling *Great Christian Prayers*. I immediately replied, "Louise can do that—that will be her book."

And so it is—this is really Louise's book. She has done all the hard work—the research and the editing. My role has been mainly to contact some contemporary Christian leaders to see if they too would like to have a part in this book. Most have responded with at least one prayer. Those who declined said they didn't write out their own prayers. I pushed a few of them to give it a try anyway—and it worked. David Yonggi Cho's secretary kindly took one of his public prayers from a tape recorder and translated it for us. So many of the prayers by Christians still living have a story of their own. It is Louise, though, who is responsible for the choice of the old prayers that constitute the bulk of this book.

The prayer attributed to George Washington may or may not have been written by him, but he certainly prayed it, as it was found in his own handwriting among his papers. In December 1994 I asked Rodney Howard-Browne if he would come to Westminster Chapel on a Saturday morning and pray in the pulpit (with no one present) and then pray for Louise. This is described in *The Anointing: Yesterday, Today, Tomorrow* (Charisma House, 2003). For over three years Louise suffered from a very serious condition that was instantly healed that day when Rodney and his wife, Adonica, laid their hands on her and prayed for her. The prayer Rodney prayed in the pulpit moments before was actually a written prayer that came out of the Welsh Revival. The memory of that day makes the prayer doubly special to us.

You might also like to read Billy Graham's response to this book:

> You and Louise have taken on a big task to pull together a book of prayers from throughout history. I do not feel qualified to be a part of such a book, but if you have a suitable spot for it—the prayer which I have perhaps been the most well-known for is that prayed at the end

of every one of our crusade meetings around the world as we invite people to receive Christ as Savior and Lord.

Because this is so basic and simple, I doubt that this is the kind of prayer you had in mind, but I submit it for your consideration since it epitomizes our entire ministry through all these years, and is the first prayer that many people ever pray as they reach out to God and begin a new life with Him.

We immediately decided that Billy's prayer should come on January 1, alongside Dr. George Carey's New Year's prayer.

We sincerely thank all those Christian leaders who have responded to our plea to share some of their prayers. I want to thank the family of Karl Barth, who have provided prayers never before published. In the case of these various Christian leaders, you will see how their prayers mirror their own ministry, situation, or suffering. It seems to me that their contributions have added wonderfully to our book, and we thank them sincerely.

There are some people who deserve our very deepest thanks. We begin with the Evangelical Library, where Louise spent a lot of time and which has loaned her not a few books. Our thanks go also to the Theological Library of King's College, London. We thank Victor Wong for sending the prayer that came out of China. Although sadly lost in the mail, we thank J. John for sending his collection of Greek Orthodox prayers.

Maurice Rowlandson has supplied names of a few British Christians I might not have thought of. Celia Bowring has helped Louise edit some of the prayers, and Lady Elizabeth Catherwood has been helpful in editing some of the great prayers of her father, Dr. D. Martyn Lloyd-Jones.

I thank Brian Reed, my assistant, who kindly took responsibility for compiling a glossary—no mean task. When he handed me the finished product, I found myself riveted; it reads like a *Who's Who* in the Christian church! My secretary Sheila Penton has worked with Louise and me throughout the period spent preparing this volume. We especially appreciate the encouragement of David Moloney, our editor, and also that of Charles Nettleton, director of Hodder & Stoughton.

This book is lovingly dedicated to Louise's mother, Mrs. Orville Hess, eighty-six at the time of this writing and living in Boise, Idaho. Thank you, Mother, for all you continue to mean to us.

—R. T. KENDALL
www.rtkendallministries.com

INTRODUCTION

*T*hose who do not have a liturgical background often find written prayers off-putting, for there is surely no adequate substitute for spontaneous prayer uttered in the Spirit. But if such a spontaneous prayer were also written down and printed, like those of Martyn Lloyd-Jones or David Yonggi Cho, could they not continue to be a blessing? So too with a written prayer that is born out of intimacy with God. I myself never felt attracted to read written prayer devotionally until one day in deep discouragement I found myself reading a prayer of Archbishop Cranmer. What amazed me was how timely it was, and how relevant to my own situation that day. It made me see how God uses written prayers.

Much the same thing can be said of hymns. Some people feel that only the psalms should be sung since they alone are inspired. Likewise, it could be said that we should pray only the prayers in the Bible, as in John 17 or Ephesians 3:14–21. Yet when Isaac Watts broke the mold in his day and began writing his own hymns, a new era followed for which most Christians thank God. So also can prayers of God's people—ancient and modern—feed and inspire us.

We have chosen not only what we believe to be some of the better prayers of Christians living and dead; we have also sought to cross denominational and theological lines. If the apostle Paul could say that he was a debtor to a wide variety of people (Rom. 1:14), so can all of us surely learn from those who come from opposite traditions and cultures to our own. If we don't meet with certain people here below, we will certainly do so at the throne of grace! It does not follow, however, that we are in agreement with the theology of all those represented in this book. Augustus Toplady may have got off his deathbed to fight a rumor that he and John Wesley had come to terms, but both of them are worshiping together in heaven as you read these lines.

These prayers are provided so that you can use them devotionally day by day, hence the reason for following the calendar and having at least one prayer for every day of the year. We hope they do inspire you as they have blessed us, that you too might find them timely and relevant in your day-to-day life. Our prayer is that God will be more real to you than ever and that the presence of Jesus Christ will be consciously experienced by every reader. As you read and pray your way through the following pages, please remember these words from Graham Kendrick:

> To keep your lovely face
> Ever before my eyes,
> This is my prayer,
> Make it my strong desire;
> That in my secret heart
> No other love competes,
> No rival throne survives,
> And I serve only You.

JANUARY 1

*O*God, I am a sinner; I am sorry for my sin; I am willing to turn from my sin. I receive Christ as Savior; I confess Him as Lord; I want to follow Him, and serve Him, in the fellowship of His church. In Christ's name. Amen.

—BILLY GRAHAM

*E*ternal God, I place myself into Your hands this coming year. May we walk together, hand in hand, and in my actions may Your will be done. Amen.

—GEORGE CAREY

JANUARY 2

My Lord and Savior, I recall
when first I heard Your voice,
Your knock;
and opened that shut door to take You at Your
     word.
As the years pass I ask myself
—and I ask You to show me—
whether my fellowship has deepened, my love
     matured,
or whether I have indeed
grown cold—a burnt-out fire?

One thing I know:
Your love remains the same.
Make it then, if there is no other way,
a chastening love leading towards repentance,
rekindling love in me.

What a lot of words, Lord Jesus,
for a simple prayer!
Be Master of my house,
its hearth and warmth,
its light and sun,
its feast and comfort,
its purpose and its joy:
for Your Name's sake. Amen.

—TIMOTHY DUDLEY-SMITH

JANUARY 3

Late have I loved Thee, O Thou Eternal Truth and Goodness; late have I sought Thee, my Father! But Thou didst seek me, and when Thou shinedst forth upon me, then I knew Thee and learnt to love Thee. I thank Thee, O my Light, that Thou didst thus shine upon me; that Thou didst teach my soul what Thou wouldst be to me, and didst incline Thy face in pity unto me; Thou, Lord, hast become my Hope, my Comfort, my Strength, my All. In Thee doth my soul rejoice. The darkness vanished from before mine eyes, and I beheld Thee, the Sun of Righteousness. When I loved darkness, I knew Thee not, but wandered on from night to night. But Thou didst lead me out of that blindness; Thou didst take me by the hand and call me to Thee, and now I can thank Thee, and Thy mighty voice that hath penetrated to my inmost heart. Amen.

—St. Augustine of Hippo

I thank Thee

JANUARY 4

O my Lord, in Thine arms I am safe; keep me, and I have nothing to fear; give me up, and I have nothing to hope for. I know nothing about the future, but I rely upon Thee. I pray Thee to give me what is good for me; I pray Thee to take from me whatever may imperil my salvation. I leave it all to Thee, because Thou knowest and I do not. If Thou bringest pain or sorrow on me, give me grace to bear it well, keep me from fretfulness and selfishness. If Thou givest me health and strength and success in this world, keep me ever on my guard lest these great gifts carry me away from Thee. Give me to know Thee, to believe on Thee, to love Thee, to serve Thee, to live to and for Thee. Give me to die just at that time and in that way that is most for Thy glory. Amen.

—JOHN HENRY NEWMAN

JANUARY 5

*B*e not weary of me, good Lord, and let me not be weary of myself, or of trying to conquer myself. I am all weakness. But Thou art almighty, and can put forth Thy strength perfectly in my weakness. Make me truly to hate all that You hate, fervently to love all that You love; make me truly sorry, for love of You, that I have so often offended You, and so mightily transform me, through Your grace, that I may no more offend You; through Jesus Christ. Amen.

—EDWARD B. PUSEY

Your Grace

JANUARY 6

Inspired by Ephesians 1:3–18

All glorious God, we give You thanks;
in Your Son Jesus Christ You have given us every
    spiritual blessing in the heavenly realms.
You chose us, before the world was made,
    to be Your holy people, without fault in Your sight.
You adopted us as Your children in Christ.
You have set us free by His blood,
    You have forgiven our sins.
You have made known to us Your secret purpose,
    to bring heaven and earth into unity in Christ.
You have given us Your Holy Spirit,
    the seal and pledge of our inheritance.
All praise and glory be Yours, O God,
    for the richness of Your grace,
    for the splendor of Your gifts,
    for the wonder of Your love.

—DESMOND TUTU

JANUARY 7

*L*ord Jesus, help me to see what it really means to have You living in me. You feel through my emotions, hurt in my body; these things that they do to me, they do to You, too. You say, "The insults that are hurled at you have fallen on Me." Lord, when they smash my life, they smash Your life, too. When they insult me, they insult You in me. When they steal my reputation and good name, they steal Your honor, too. I know You feel angry for me and will fight on my behalf. Help me to rest in that fact. They rejected You, insulted and humiliated You as well, as they hit You over and over again. Yet You still forgave. O Jesus, forgive me for not forgiving, too—help me love my enemy as You loved Yours.

—Jennifer Rees Larcombe

O Lord, who hast given us Thy sun to gladden us with light and to ripen the fruits of the earth for our support, and to set when his work is done, that he may rise again tomorrow; give Thy blessing to us Thy servants, that the lesson of the works of Thy hand may be learnt by us Thy living works, and that we may run our course like the sun which is now gone from us.

Let us rise early and go late to rest, being ever busy and zealous in doing Thy will. Let our light shine before men, that they may glorify Thee, our Heavenly Father. Let us do good all our days, and be useful to and comfort others. And let us finish our course in faith, that we too may rise again to a course which shall never end.

—THOMAS ARNOLD

Let our light shine before men

NOVEMBER 20

My heavenly Daddy, every time I come into your presence to say "thank You," I feel that these two words are so inadequate in the light of the overwhelming blessings You have poured out on me through Your beloved Son and my Lord, Jesus Christ. Yet I am comforted in the knowledge that You know the depth of my gratitude to You for:

+ Living in this great country
+ A godly wife and children who love You
+ The privilege of ministering in Your name
+ Friends and Christian fellowship

But above all of these great blessings, precious Father, I am thankful for:

+ My salvation
+ Raising me from the tomb of spiritual death and sin
+ Forgiving me of *all* of my sins
+ Relieving me from the pain and torment of guilt
+ Giving me the assurance of eternity in heaven with You and my Lord, Jesus

How can I thank You for all of this?

I will thank You daily, not only with my lips, but also with my time, with my talent, and with my treasure. Amen.

—MICHAEL YOUSSEF

O Lord God, we bless thee, for Jesus Christ and His great salvation, for the covenant of grace made with us in Him, and for all the exceeding great and precious promises and privileges of that covenant; for the throne of grace to which we may come in His name with humble boldness, and for the blessed hope of eternal life through Him. We confess that we have sinned and done foolishly. O Lord, Thou knowest our foolishness, and our sins are not hidden from Thee. Who can understand his errors; O cleanse Thou us from our secret faults.

We pray Thee to give us repentance for our sins and make us sensible of the evil of them, and let the blood of Christ cleanse us from them.

—MATTHEW HENRY

The depth of my gratitude to You

NOVEMBER 22

*L*ord, the creatures of Thy hand, Thy children, come before Thee with their wishes and regrets: Children we are, children we shall be, till our mother the earth hath fed upon our bones. Accept us, correct us, guide us, Thy guilty innocents. Dry our vain tears, wipe out our vain resentments, help our yet vainer efforts. Be patient still; suffer us yet awhile longer—with our broken purposes of good, with our idle endeavors against evil, suffer us awhile longer to endure, and (if it may be) help us to do better. We thank Thee and praise Thee.

—ROBERT LOUIS STEVENSON

*G*lory to our ascended Lord that He is with us always.

Glory to the Word of God, going forth with His armies conquering and to conquer.

Glory to Him who has led captivity captive and given gifts for the perfecting of His saints.

Glory to Him who has gone before to prepare a place in His Father's home for us.

Glory to the Author and Finisher of our faith; that God in all things may be glorified through Jesus Christ,

To whom be all worship and praise, dominion, and glory; now and for ever and ever. Amen.

—SURSUM CORDA

NOVEMBER 24

O Light eternal, transcending all created suns, cause Thy bright beams to shine into our hearts. Purify, warm, enlighten, and quicken our souls with all their powers: so that they may find their rest, their joy, in Thee.

The days of this present life are short and evil, full of troubles and sorrows: when wilt Thou bring the reign of Satan to an end: and grant to us to walk at liberty, without trials or temptations, seeing Thy face, and wearing Thy likeness? Until then, preserve us, O Thou eternal Truth; come unto us, O heavenly Love; draw our affections away from earthly things, and fix them upon Thyself. Blessed are they, O Lord, whom Thou choosest, and whom Thou causest to approach unto Thee.

—THOMAS À KEMPIS

*G*rant, O heavenly Father, that we so faithfully believe in Thee, and so fervently love one another, always living in Thy fear, and in the obedience of Thy holy law and blessed will, that we, being fruitful in all good works, may lead our life according to Thy good pleasure in this world and, after this frail and short life, obtain the true and immortal life, where Thou livest and reignest, world without end. Amen.

—THOMAS BECON

O merciful Lord, of Thy bountiful goodness, receive us evermore into Thy protection, maintaining and increasing from day to day Thy grace and goodness towards us, until Thou hast brought us unto the full and perfect unity of Thy Son, Jesus Christ our Lord, who is the true light of our souls.

—LITURGY OF GENEVA

Thy good pleasure

NOVEMBER 26

*L*ord Jesus Christ, grant me Your special grace to speak Your Truth in love and to challenge every way that would exclude Love from Truth or Truth from Love. You who are both Truth and Love, enter my poor heart and mind afresh to bring forth this miracle of Truthful Love and Loving Truth for which I pray in Your most worthy Name. Amen.

—MICHAEL CASSIDY

*C*ome, Holy Spirit, and daily increase in us Thy manifold gifts of grace; the spirit of wisdom and understanding; the spirit of counsel and ghostly strength; the spirit of knowledge and true godliness, and fill us with the spirit of Thy holy fear, now and for ever. Amen.

—GELASIAN SACRAMENTARY

*F*ather, I want to be like You. I want my heart to be as big as Yours.

As far as revival is concerned, I ask You to find those who will be guileless and entrust them with the wonderful treasures of Your power and Your presence. Please don't hide from us because our hearts are divided. Make us one big family rejoicing in Your love.

Lord, I hunger for Your Word, but I don't believe that knowing You is only about memorizing Scripture or learning about how You've moved in the past. Knowing all that is valuable only if I can trust You like a little child.

I'm so glad, Father, that loving You with a childlike spirit is all that is necessary to please You, and knowing that makes me love You more.

—JOHN ARNOTT

*L*ord, live so completely within me that all my life will be the natural outpouring of the divine power—the consequence of an indwelling Spirit of purity and truth.

—WALTER JAMES

NOVEMBER 28

Loving heavenly Father, hallowed be Thy name, Thou art from everlasting to everlasting, the Father of my Savior the Lord Jesus Christ and one with the Holy Spirit in the blessed Trinity. I come boldly but reverently into Your holy presence in the name of Jesus. I come to You washed in the blood of the Lamb and knowing that I am holy and blameless in Your sight, O God, by Your altogether lovely Lord Jesus. I love You with all my heart, soul, and mind. I am unworthy of Your love, mercy, and long-suffering. You have been generous to my family and me. Grant, I beseech, every gift of the Holy Spirit according to Your sovereign will that I may lift up the name of Jesus for His glory alone. I confess I have sinned in word, thought, and deed, that I have been unfaithful in the face of Your faithfulness to me. Wash me in the blood of the Lamb for I am truly sorry for my sins. Renew in me the joy of my salvation. Grant me wisdom according to Your promise, integrity, and compassion that I may be fitted to serve You in the fulfillment of the Great Commission until Jesus comes to calls me home. All this I pray in the name of Jesus. Amen.

—GRAHAM F. LACEY

O Lord, enable me to live the life of saints and angels. Take me out of the irritability, the sensitiveness, in which my soul lies, and fill it with Thy fullness.

Breathe on me with that Breath which infuses energy and kindles fervor. In asking for fervor, I ask for all that I can need, and all that Thou canst give. In asking for fervor, I am asking for faith, hope, and charity, in their most heavenly exercise; I am asking for perception of duty, I am asking for sanctity, peace, and joy, all at once. Nothing would be a trouble to me, nothing a difficulty, had I but a fervor of soul. Lord, in asking for fervor, I am asking for Thyself, for nothing short of Thee, O my God. Enter my heart, and fill it with fervor by filling it with Thee. Amen.

—JOHN HENRY NEWMAN

Lift up the name of Jesus

Dear heavenly Father, while I am on this journey through life, I pray that I may always listen for Your voice, whether it is for praise or discipline. Please, please may I always know Your presence, especially if I am to journey through life's valleys. When I am weak fill me with Your strength, and help me to love like You love, even when it hurts. May nothing matter to me more than becoming the person You want me to be. Amen.

—DIANNE PARSONS

DECEMBER 1

Father, thank You for Your reliability; for the energy of Your Holy Spirit that causes the sun to rise. Thank You for the potential of this new day. Thank You that You have called and chosen me to work for You today and the power that causes the sun to rise is the same power that is at work by Your Holy Spirit in my life. Let me not shrink back from anything today, but complete the work You have already ordained for me to do…following the course You have set, not veering to the right or the left. May my heart beat in time with Yours. May I see through Your eyes. May I hear with understanding. Give me the determination and singlemindedness to keep sight of the vision and finish the job.

—JULIA FISHER

DECEMBER 2

*H*ave pity upon us, O Lord, and look down upon us from the throne of Thy majesty; scatter the darkness of our souls, and enlighten us with the beams of Thy Holy Spirit.

Give us wisdom to discern between good and evil. Above all, we entreat of Thee full and free remission of all our sins; for Thou, O Lord Jesus, hast died to purchase it.

Lord, we pray Thee to bestow upon us everlasting life, not for our merits, but for Thy great mercy: upon which we cast ourselves as the only refuge and hope of sinners. Lord Jesus, hear us; heavenly Father, be merciful unto us; Holy Spirit, comfort us; and to Thy name, O blessed and holy Trinity, shall be praise and glory for ever and ever. Amen.

—St. Augustine of Hippo

DECEMBER 3

You know me, Lord, my down-sitting and my uprising, and You are acquainted with all my ways—the good, the bad, and the indifferent, the right, the wrong, the holy, the sinful, the ones that make You happy and the ones that make You sad. Lord, I read Your Word and it says: "I have seen his ways, BUT I will heal him." You do know my ways and how far they fall short of Your holiness, but nevertheless in grace and mercy You will heal me. Thank You, Lord. To be sure I can rest in nothing but the "buts" of God and the "But God…" words of a heavenly Father full of grace and mercy for undeserving sinners such as I.

Thank You, Lord, yes, thank You. Amen and amen.

—MICHAEL CASSIDY

DECEMBER 4

O Lord Jesus, great is Thy goodness to them that seek Thee. Thou redeemest the captives; Thou art the Savior of the lost, the strength of the weary, the freedom of the oppressed, the consolation of them that are cast down, the crown of the conquering, the reward and joy of Thy saints. O mighty God, may all things that are in heaven above and in the earth beneath bless Thee, for Thou art great, and great is Thy name. When Thou shalt come in Thy power and glory, raise us up, we beseech Thee, among Thy chosen, that in our flesh we may see Thy brightness, and be filled with the joy of Thy countenance.

—ANSELM

Thou art great

DECEMBER 5

Almighty God, I read that at the beginning it was dark. But suddenly You said, "Let there be light." And there was light. The world had never known the sun or the moon. It was as dark as it ever has been. But You decided it was time for light. No warning, no argument, no battle against the host of darkness. Just a decision.

At times for me the darkness is suffocation—it threatens to swamp me, sap me of hope, wear me down with its heaviness. But in heaven You watch. And when You decide the time is right the piercing light can come—in a moment. Lord, lighten my darkness.

—ROB PARSONS

DECEMBER 6

Forgive me, Lord, that my prayers are often nearly all asking, with too little praising. Yet I thank You that even this praises You because I trust only in Your faithfulness and steadfast love. Help me to fix my eyes upon You and make Your glory the starting point of prayer, that my expectancy may know no limits.

Teach me when to be silent before You and when to speak, not missing hearing You through my eagerness to speak without listening. May I come in awe, because of Your greatness, and joy as I relax in Your presence, calling You "Abba, Father."

As I read Your Word reveal the truth about Yourself, that I may praise You more and more. Amen.

—DEREK PRIME

I come in awe

*L*ord, nevertheless I am continually with You, although Your way is hidden from me. I know You uphold me with Your right hand. You lead me according to Your counsel, even when I see nothing but darkness. You make a path in the wilderness and cause me to reach the goal. Lord, I am ashamed that I was so defeated. Help me to realize Your sustaining presence is always there.

—CORRIE TEN BOOM

DECEMBER 8

*T*here is no holiness, O Lord, if Thou withdraw Thine hand.

We are weak in ourselves, but strong in Thee; we are cold, till Thou warmest us with the warmth of life.

Blessed Jesus, grant us Thy grace; may it work with us, and in us, and continue with us to the end. Teach us to desire always that which is acceptable to Thee. Grant us to rest in Thee, and to enjoy in Thee that peace which the world cannot give.

—THOMAS À KEMPIS

*L*ook down upon Thy servants with a patient eye, even as Thou sendest sun and rain: look down, quicken, enliven; re-create in us the soul of service, the spirit of peace; renew in us the sense of joy.

—ROBERT LOUIS STEVENSON

December 9

*H*eavenly Father, how grateful we are for Your steadfast love toward us when You could have justly abandoned us because of our rebellion and indifference toward You. We deserved to be excluded from Your presence forever and yet You came to visit us, clothed Yourself with our humanity, experienced our earthly pain, and even died, sacrificed Yourself in order to save us. How privileged we are to be embraced with Your love, to have received Your forgiveness, to know Your peace and to be called Your children. Forgive us for our lack of moral courage to speak to friends and neighbors of Your great love for them. We are ashamed that too often we are more concerned about our reputation than other people's salvation. Forgive us that we are so easily deceived by people's outward prosperity and apparent happiness that we no longer see them as lost, perishing, and without hope.

—Victor Jack

DECEMBER 10

O God our Father, we thank Thee for all Thy loving care, and for giving us so many good things to enjoy; send us on our way now to do our duty through this day. Grant that we may always stand firm on the side of right, and spread Thy kingdom of happiness with Thee and the Holy Spirit, one God, world without end. Amen.

—PERCY DEARMER

O Christ, the Sun of Righteousness, who didst manifest Thyself in our flesh, shine graciously into our hearts, that, walking as children of light, we may glorify Thee before men, and being always ready to obey Thy call, may, in our place, hold up the light of life to them that sit in darkness and the shadow of death. Hear us, O Lord, for Thy great mercies' sake, who livest and reignest with the Father and the Holy Ghost, now and for ever. Amen.

—HENRY STOBART

DECEMBER 11

O Holy Spirit, who art Thyself the love with which the Father loves His Son and the Son loves the Father, let the love that Thou art fill our hearts that we may share in the communion of the Father and the Son, and from that communion go forth to minister in the name and likeness of Jesus Christ our Lord.

—THOMAS TORRANCE

Almighty God, who seest that we have no power of ourselves to help ourselves: keep us both outwardly in our bodies, and inwardly in our souls; that we may be defended from all adversities which may happen to the body, and from all evil thoughts which may assault and hurt the soul; through Jesus Christ our Lord. Amen.

—GREGORIAN SACRAMENTARY

DECEMBER 12

Our Father, I know well Thou canst never forsake those who seek Thee, nor disappoint those who trust Thee. Yet I know too, the more I pray for Thy protection, the more surely and fully I shall have it. And therefore now I cry out to Thee, first that Thou wouldest keep me from myself, and from following any will but Thine. Next, I beg of Thee, O my loving Lord—if it be not wrong so to pray—visit me not with those trying visitations which saints alone can bear! Pity my weakness, and lead me heavenwards in a safe and tranquil course. Still I leave all in Thy hands—only, if Thou shalt bring heavier trials on me, give me more grace, flood me with the fullness of Thy strength and consolation. Amen.

—JOHN HENRY NEWMAN

I leave all in Thy hands

DECEMBER 13

*G*od of all compassion, whose will is that none should perish in their sins but that all should come to repentance; have mercy upon the millions who have never heard of the saving grace of our Lord Jesus Christ, or who, having heard, have failed to respond to the gospel.

Turn the tide of evil in our land and in lands across the world, that unbelief and ignorance of Your Word and will may be transformed, and that men and women, loving You above all else, may learn to love each other. Purge from Your world the hatred and inhumanity, the contempt and the violence.

—KEITH WESTON

DECEMBER 14

*L*ord, often when I am longing to talk with my husband the phone rings or he's off to another church meeting. Please give me patience and wisdom to carve out time together.

It's wearing being short of money and needing the whole PCC to agree before we replace the washing machine (which was probably salvaged from the ark anyway). Please give me patience and wisdom about that, too.

And when people criticize us and our ministry, I feel it so keenly and get lonely and depressed. Please send a friend I can share with, and thank You for all the kindness and love our congregation gives.

We're in this ministry together, as a couple, as a family. Every day we need Your help. Thank You for bringing us here and for Your promise to be with us, always. Amen.

—CELIA BOWRING

We have rested under

DECEMBER 15

O loving God, we thank Thee once more for the quiet rest of the night that has gone by, for the new promise that has come with this fresh morning, and for the hope of this day. While we have slept, the world in which we live has swept on in its awful space, great waters have been all about us, and great storms above us: but Thou hast held them back by Thy strong hand, and we have rested under the shadow of Thy love. The bird sat on the spray out in the darkness, the flower nestled in the grass, we lay down in our home, and all slept in the arms of God. The bird will trust Thee this day to give its morsel of meat, and the flower will trust Thee for its fresh raiment; so may we trust Thee this day for all the needs of the body, the soul, and the spirit. Amen.

—ROBERT COLLYER

the shadow of Your love

DECEMBER 16

*L*ord, I'm a bit of a struggler.

In fact, I struggle far more than I ever dreamt I would. I struggle with life, and in my relationship with You, other people, and even with myself.

Lord, I'm a bit of a doubter.

In fact, I doubt more than I ever dreamt I would. My motives are muddled, my vision confused—more than I like to acknowledge.

Lord, I'm more than a little frustrated.

In fact, I'm far more frustrated than I ever dreamt I'd be. I'm frustrated with myself for not listening. Worse yet, though I hardly dare admit it, I'm sometimes frustrated with You.

Still, I do love You and want to listen to Your voice rather than mine. I want Your will to be done.

So keep sorting me out. I know You love me and forgive my inconsistencies. That's why I'm here and trust You. And that's why I'm not going anywhere else.

—STEVE CHALKE

Increase my faith

DECEMBER 17

*D*earest Lord, may I see You today and every day in the person of Your sick, and while nursing them, minister to You.

Even when You hide Yourself behind the unattractive disguise of the irritable, the exacting, the unreasonable, may I still recognize You and gladly serve You.

O Jesus, bear with my faults, and look only at my intention, which is to love and serve You in the person of each of Your sick. Lord, increase my faith, and bless my efforts and work, now and for evermore.

—MOTHER TERESA

*O*Father Almighty; O Lord Jesus the Son of the Father; O Holy Spirit who proceedest from the Father and the Son, keep, we pray Thee, these creatures of Thy hand; who put their trust in Thee, and take refuge in Thy mercy.

—ST. AUGUSTINE OF HIPPO

DECEMBER 18

Father in the Highest, who hast promised to dwell with them that are of a lowly spirit and fear Thy Word; create now in us such lowly hearts, and give us a reverential awe of Thy commandments. O come, Thou Holy Spirit, and kindle our hearts with holy love; come, Thou Spirit of Strength, and arouse our souls to hunger and thirst after Thee, their true Guide, that they may be sustained by Thy all-powerful influence.

—GERHARD TERSTEEGEN

O God, who hast prepared for them that love Thee such good things as pass man's understanding, pour into our hearts such love towards Thee, that we, loving Thee above all things, may obtain Thy promises, which exceed all that we can desire; through Jesus Christ our Lord. Amen.

—GELASIAN SACRAMENTARY

DECEMBER 19

Heavenly Father, whose Son Jesus Christ ministered full of grace and truth, help us so to receive Him that we might increasingly reflect Him. His truth has set us free and upon His grace we depend from start to finish of our Christian lives. Enable us to defend the truth, proclaim the truth, and live by the truth. Inspire us to do all in the spirit of gracious love so that Jesus may be seen in us.

We pray for Your church worldwide that it may never waver from the truth of the gospel. We pray for rebuke and restoration where it has gone astray, and we ask that Your people in these days may mirror the grace and truth of their Savior and Lord Jesus Christ. Amen.

—PHILIP HACKING

DECEMBER 20

*L*ord, again we thank Thee for Thy Word. We are prone to wander, detracting and subtracting from it, making things easy for ourselves, but we bless Thee for this Word, teaching and instructing us, warning and safeguarding us from the subtle assaults of the enemy who appears as an angel of light to twist and pervert even Thy holy Word.

Lord, we thank Thee for the faith we have; may Thou grant more clear assurance so we may give diligence to making our election sure. Thou has provided the way for this. Grant that Your dear children may know as never before the Spirit bearing witness with them that they are the children of God, through Christ our Lord. Amen.

—D. MARTYN LLOYD-JONES

DECEMBER 21

Lord our God, thank You for all the love that our Lord Jesus Christ showed, while on earth, to those in need, the sick, the hungry, the outcasts. Help us to follow His example and, because of our love for You, and because He has commanded us, to love our neighbor as ourselves.

Lord, we know that if we do not show Your love in our own lives, no one will believe in the God of love whom we preach; that if we care for the needs they feel, they may listen when we tell them of their greatest need of all, which they do not yet feel.

So Lord, as we feel Your great love for us in sending Your Son to die for us and His love in bearing our sin and being separated from You, may we feel that same love for our fellow men and women, all created by You in Your image.

—SIR FRED CATHERWOOD

We feel Your great love

DECEMBER 22

*W*e come unto our fathers' God. Their Rock is our Foundation. O Thou God of our fathers, be, we beseech Thee, the Guide of their succeeding race....In this hour of restlessness and turmoil lead us into the secret place. Lift us above the clash of the hour. The air is charged with calamity and our hearts are strangely moved. Make Thy way manifest, even though overtures of peace have broken down. In the hour of our extremity we turn to Thee....If it be decreed in the awful and perfect counsel of Thy holy will, that we can be purged and redeemed only through suffering, grant to all of us who bear Thy holy Name a quietness and resignation of Spirit such as shall make us strong in the hour of our chastisement!

—G. CAMPBELL MORGAN

DECEMBER 23

*D*ear Lord, we claim again the joy we need to overcome our sins and sorrows and the thorns which infest our ground.

And do make Your blessings flow to wherever any curse or curses may be found.

In Your Name, O Lord, and by Your power, we break all curses directed at us or our loved ones.

We record them this day as broken.

And neutralized.

And banished.

And may we all now go out and prevail as far as the curse is found.

In Jesus' strong and all-prevailing name we pray. Amen.

—MICHAEL CASSIDY

Lead us into the secret place

A marvelous wonder has come to pass:
Nature is made new, and God becomes man.
That which He was, He has remained;
And that which He was not, He has taken on
     Himself
While suffering neither confusion nor division.
How shall I tell of this great mystery?
He who is without flesh becomes incarnate;
The Word puts on a body;
The Invisible is seen;
He whom no hand can touch is handled;
And He who has no beginning now begins to be.
The Son of God becomes the Son of man:
Jesus Christ, the same yesterday, today, and for
     ever.

—THE ORTHODOX WAY
CHRISTMAS DAY VESPERS

*The Word puts
on a body*

December 25

O God, grant us to know that the One born of old in Bethlehem has also been born in our hearts; a living Christ within, never leaving us. O Lord, follow us to our homes, our work, wherever we go and in whatever we do. May we know Thou wilt never forsake us, and witness the sweet intimations of Thy nearness and grace.

Bless, O God, those who long to know Thee better and the truth more truly. And now, may the grace of our Lord and Savior Jesus Christ, the love of God and the fellowship of the Holy Spirit abide with us throughout the remainder of this our short and uncertain earthly pilgrimage and for ever more. Amen.

—D. Martyn Lloyd-Jones

DECEMBER 26

Glory be to God in the highest, and on earth peace, goodwill towards men. We praise Thee, we bless Thee, we glorify Thee, we give thanks unto Thee, for this greatest of Thy mercies, O Lord God, heavenly King, God the Father Almighty. O Lord, the only begotten Son Jesus Christ, O Lord God, Lamb of God, Son of the Father, who wast made man to take away the sins of the world, have mercy upon us by turning us from our iniquities. Thou who wast manifested to destroy the works of the devil, have mercy upon us by enabling us to renounce and forsake them. Thou who art the great Advocate with the Father, receive our prayer, we humbly beseech Thee. Amen.

—THOMAS KEN

December 27

How excellent is Thy mercy, O God!
And the children of men shall put their trust
under the shadow of Thy wings.
The Lord bless us, and keep us,
and show the light of His countenance upon us,
and be merciful unto us.
The Lord lift up His countenance upon us,
And give us peace!
I commend to Thee, O Lord,
my soul and my body,
my mind and my thoughts,
my prayers and my vows,
my senses and my limbs,
my words and my works,
my life and my death.
Hear, O Lord, and have mercy upon me;
Lord, be Thou my helper.

—Lancelot Andrewes

DECEMBER 28

We thank Thee, Lord Jesus, that Thou, our High Priest before the throne of God, art ever living to make intercession for us. We thank Thee that Thou art touched with the feeling of our infirmity, and hast been in all points tempted like as we are yet without sin. Help us therefore to come boldly to Thy throne of Grace that we may obtain mercy, and find grace to help in time of need. Help us to watch and pray that we enter not into temptation. Strengthen our weakness by Thy divine strength, so shall we render to Thee, Lord Jesus, with the Father and the Holy Ghost, all honor and praise now and for evermore. Amen.

—MATTHEW HENRY

DECEMBER 29

*L*ord, when I die, the only things I want to leave behind are souls that are saved, lives that are happier, and situations that are better. Grant this, I pray, in Jesus' Name.

—MICHAEL CASSIDY

*L*ord, grant that my last hour may be my best hour.

—A. S. T. FISHER

All honor and praise now and forevermore

DECEMBER 30

*L*ord, help us to rise clean out of this world and its down-dragging tendencies, towards Thyself. We do not ask to be entranced by shining angels, but for Thy presence, Jesus, to be as if our eyes behold Thee and our fingers touched Thy nail prints. Thou hast ransomed Thy people with Thy heart's blood. Risen, ascended through the gates of pearl to Thy Father's throne we seem to see Thee, our ears almost catching the everlasting song rolling up at Thy feet. Over angelic squadrons Thou lookest and hearest our praises. Best Beloved, we have no one in heaven but Thee; none upon earth we desire besides Thee. Father, Son, and Holy Ghost accept us and in Jesus' name. Amen.

—CHARLES H. SPURGEON

Be among us and remain with

DECEMBER 31

May the fire of Christ consume all
   indifference to God
The light of Christ illumine our vision of God
The love of Christ enlarge our longing for God
The Spirit of Christ empower our service to
   God
And the blessing of God Almighty,
The Father, the Son, and the Holy Spirit
Be among us, and remain with us always.

—JAMES JONES

us always

ACKNOWLEDGMENTS

*W*hile the authors and publisher have made every effort to contact the copyright holders of material used in this book, this has not always been successful. Full acknowledgment will gladly be made in future editions.

We gratefully acknowledge the following, extracts from which appear in this book:

Congregational Union of England and Wales. *Book of Congregational Worship.* N.p.: Turnbull and Spears, 1920.

Dudley-Smith, Timothy. *Someone Who Beckons.* Westmont, IL: InterVarsity Press, 1978.

Kendrick, Graham. "To Keep Your Lovely Face." Copyright © 1983 Thank You Music. Admin. by EMI Christian Music Publishing. All rights reserved. Used by permission.

———. "I Kneel Down." Copyright © 1998 Make Way Music. Admin. by Music Services in the Western Hemisphere. All rights reserved. ASCAP. Used by permission.

Larcombe, Jennifer Rees. *Turning Point.* London: Hodder and Stoughton, 1994.

Lawrence, Brother. *The Practice of the Presence of God,* trans. E. M. Blaiklock. London: Hodder and Stoughton, 1981.

Prime, Derek. *Created to Praise.* Belleville, MI: Christian Focus Publications, 1981.

Redpath, Alan. *Victorians Praying.* N.p.: Pickering and Inglis, 1957.

Robinson, Godfrey and Stephen Winward. *Scripture Union Prayer Book*. N.p.: Scripture Union, 1967.

Slater, William. *The Song of the Salvation Army*. N.p.: The Salvation Army, 1953.

Scott, John. *Your Confirmation*. London: Hodder and Stoughton, 1991.

ten Boom, Corrie. *This Day Is the Lord's*. London: Hodder and Stoughton, 1980.

Tutu, Desmond. *An African Prayer Book*. London: Hodder and Stoughton, 1996.

Ware, Timothy. *The Orthodox Church*. New York: Penguin Books, 1963.

Weatherhead, Leslie. *A Private House of Prayer*. London: Hodder and Stoughton, 1958.

GLOSSARY

Acts of Devotion—Devotional prayer book published in 1914. 195

Alcuin of York (c. 732–804)—Master of York Cathedral School; Charlemagne's tutor and counselor; established schools and libraries in France; poet; abbot of Tours. 220

Alford, Henry (1810–1871)—Born in Middlesex, he dedicated his life to God at the age of sixteen; Anglican minister in Wiltshire, Leicestershire and London—becoming Dean of Canterbury Cathedral in 1857; wrote hymns, including "Come, Ye Thankful People, Come." 227, 258

Amess, Robert (1944–)—Born in Bristol, he has been pastor of several churches in the UK, including Duke Street Baptist Church, Richmond. He is now the chairman of the Evangelical Alliance. 140

Andrewes, Lancelot (1565–1626)—Anglican bishop of Ely and, later, Winchester; dean of the Royal Chapel to James I; now best known for his *Manual of Private Devotion and Meditation for the Visitation of the Sick*; involved in the King James Version translation team for parts of the Old Testament. 25, 50, 123, 175, 204, 248, 263, 275, 293, 373

Anselm (1035–1109)—Born in Italy, he was awakened to a love of holy things and religious ideas by his mother when he was fifteen, and thereafter sought to conform to God's will; philosopher and theologian; developed the argument for the eternal self-existence of the divine nature known as the Ontological argument; reluctant archbishop of Canterbury in 1093; known for his guileless simplicity, integrity, faithful zeal, and patient suffering for righteousness' sake. 26, 57, 120, 201, 264, 268, 350

Apostolic Constitutions—Multi-volume liturgical prayer book, written around 325 to 400. 56, 191, 288, 304

Aquinas, St. Thomas (1224–1274)—Dominican theologian, born in Italy; was placed in his uncle's monastery at the age of five; master of theology; stressed that Christian revelation and human knowledge are facets of a single truth and cannot be in conflict. 203

Arndt, Johann (1555–1621)—German Lutheran minister who sought to restore the moral climate among German Protestants; wrote *One True Christianity*, a study of religious and practical influence on moral conduct (a book much valued by Wesley), and *The Garden of Paradise*, a book of prayers and spiritual exercises. 127

Arnold, Dr. Thomas (1795–1842)—Known as "Poet Arnold" when young; chaplain, then headmaster of Rugby School; sought to bring religion into the daily concern of men and to invest every act of life with a Christian character. 210, 335

Arnott, John (1940–)—Born in Toronto, Canada, where he is now the senior pastor of Toronto Airport Christian Fellowship which he founded in 1988; special emphasis on the Father heart of God; author of a number of books including *The Father's Blessing*; television broadcaster with a worldwide evangelistic and healing ministry. 86, 343

Athanasius, St. (c. 296–373)—Archbishop of Alexandria, who stood alone as the "Champion of Orthodoxy," even against the emperor; stood against Arianism; under his influence, the Council of Nicea acknowledged the eternity of the Word of God and the Divinity of Christ—this was at a price, though, and St. Athanasius spent much time in exile in the Egyptian desert. 294

Augustine of Hippo, St. (354–430)— Born in Algeria; trained as a lawyer but turned to philosophy and renounced his early Christian training; after a long inner conflict (see *Confessions*), Augustine was converted and baptized in 386 and ordained in 391; returned to North Africa and became bishop of Hippo; he was known as Doctor of Grace; few, if any, Christian writers have written with equal depth on charity and on the Holy Trinity; created a theology that has remained basic to western Christianity ever since. 14, 19, 43, 66, 83, 111, 149, 174, 202, 208, 230, 311, 320, 348, 363

Balfour, Doug (1958–)—Doug was born in north London, and is now general director of Tearfund; he has been an explorational geologist, relief worker, missionary with YWAM, management consultant and stockbroker; he is married with three children and lives in west London. 277

Barth, Karl (1886–1968)—Swiss Protestant theologian and pastor; professor at Basel; stood for the primacy of the gospel against the demands of the Nazi state. He was possibly the greatest theologian of the twentieth century. 41, 142, 282

Basil, St. (330–379)—Bishop of Caesarea, theologian, monastic founder and teacher; was a bishop of remarkable ability—he distributed his inheritance to the poor during a famine and organized a soup kitchen; father of Greek monasticism, with an emphasis on community life, liturgical prayer, and manual work. 20

Baxter, Richard (1615–1691)—Puritan pastor, serving first as an Anglican at Kidderminster, England, before rejecting his belief in the episcopacy; leaned toward the Presbyterian position; wrote *The Reformed Pastor* in 1656. 200

Becon, Thomas (1512–1567)—Protestant divine; fellow student and friend of Hugh Latimer; wrote against corruption in the church and campaigned for the Bible to be accessible to people; Becon's writings were banned and he spent time in the Tower of London; became chaplain to Archbishop Cranmer at Canterbury. 341

Benedict, St. (480–543)—Born in Italy, lived as a hermit, then became abbot of a monastery and established twelve more monasteries including Monte Cassino; founder of the Benedictine discipline for monastic life—accepted throughout the West as centers of learning, agriculture, hospitality, and medicine, adaptable to the needs of society. 320

Benn, Rt. Rev. Wallace (1947–)— Born in Dublin, Wallace has ministered in England for twenty-eight years, including as vicar of St. Peter's, Harold Wood; he is currently bishop of Lewes; convention speaker, including at Spring Harvest; author of *The Last Word* and *Jesus Our Joy*, passionate about mission and Bible teaching. 159

Bernardine of Siena, St. (1380–1444)—Orphan, brought up by his aunt; when he was twenty, took charge of the local hospital during the plague; became a Franciscan friar, and a popular preacher in Italy based in Milan; drew very large crowds for sermons that were three to four hours long, and which resulted in numerous conversions; described as a second St. Paul; devoted to the holy name of Jesus, he used the letters IHS as Greek "shorthand" for "Jesus—Son of God—Savior"; turned down three bishoprics. 96, 97

Bersier, Eugène (1831–1889)—Minister at L'église de l'étoile, Paris; pastor and writer. 318

Bewes, Rev. Richard (1934–)—Richard was born in Kenya—his parents were missionaries; he entered the Anglican ministry and pastored at Harold Wood; Emmanuel, Northwood, and is currently rector at All Souls Church, Langham Place; he is married with three adult children, and fits tennis and photography around his work of preaching, broadcasting, and writing. 91

Bonhoeffer, Dietrich (1906–1945)—German Protestant theologian, influenced by Karl Barth; opposed Nazism from 1933 and returned to Germany from the UK to train pastors for the Confessing (anti-Nazi) church; involved in a plot to assassinate Hitler; executed in 1945; became famous for his *Letters and Papers From Prison.* 180, 244, 318

Book of Common Prayer—Worship and liturgy book of the Anglican church, compiled by Thomas Cranmer during the Reformation. 98, 130, 154, 164, 216, 224, 313, 321

Book of Congregational Prayer, 1920—Prayers and orders of worship for congregational churches. 42, 151, 158, 232, 269, 308, 319

Booth, William (1829–1912)—Converted at the age of fifteen; Methodist minister—established a mission in London's East End that was later called the Salvation Army; separated from Methodism; campaigned to alert the nation to child prostitution and child labor; established hostels and rescue houses; published *In Darkest England and the Way Out* in 1890. 154

Bowring, Celia (1952–)—Celia was born in Tripoli, Libya; she is married to Lyndon and they have three children; Celia writes the *CARE Prayer Guide*, articles in Christian magazines and Bible notes, and is

the author of *The Special Years: An Essential Guide for Parents of Under Fives.* 165, 360

Bowring, Lyndon (1948–)—Lyndon comes from Caerphilly, Wales, and was an Elim Pentecostal minister as part of the team at Kensington Temple until 1985; then he became executive chairman of CARE, an organization seeking to encourage and serve the church to engage in Christian caring, campaigning, and action. 166, 241

Buchanan, Rev. Alex (1928–)—Born in London, Alex has been minister or elder in several churches of various denominations: Brethren, Baptist, City Mission, FIEC, and Anglican; leader of Intercessors for Britain and a leader of Intercessors International; author, minister at large, pastor to Spring Harvest; describes himself as "one of God's errand boys." 173

Buchanan, Peggy (1934–)—Peggy was born in Buxton, Derbyshire, is married to Alex, and is a mother and grandmother. She was formerly a schoolteacher, but became ill with MS in 1965; currently she is a Spring Harvest speaker and travels and shares with Alex in his ministry. 212

Buxton, David (1964–)—Born in west London, David became the first deaf Borough councilor and the first born-deaf parliamentary candidate in the UK; he is a leader of organizations for the deaf in Britain, such as Breakthrough Deaf-Hearing Integration and Christian Deaf-Link UK; he travels, preaches, and teaches the Bible in the UK and overseas. 309

Calthrop, Rev. Gordon (late nineteenth century)—Vicar of St. Augustine's, Highbury, and author of the devotional books called *Family Prayers* and *The Gospel Year.* 94

Calvin, John (1509–1564)—Brilliant

teacher of Reformation theology, developing Luther's Reformation ideas; based at Geneva, Switzerland, which he decided to turn into an exemplary Christian city "to nourish and nurture the exterior service of Christ"; his works include *The Institutes of the Christian Religion*, published in 1536. 22, 84, 185, 270, 274, 313

Campolo, Dr. Tony (1955–)—Taught sociology at the university level for over thirty-five years; evangelist and leader of the mission organization EAPE/Kingdomworks, which has developed an array of ministries in urban America and in developing countries. 104

Carey, Most Rev. and Rt. Hon. George (1935–)—Born in Bow, east London, Dr. Carey has been archbishop of Canterbury since 1991; formerly principal of Trinity College, Bristol, and bishop of Bath and Wells. 12

Carmina Gadelica—A collection of prayers from the Highlands and islands of Scotland. 233

Cassidy, Dr. Michael (1936–)—Michael was born in Johannesburg, South Africa; trained at Cambridge and at the Fuller Theological Seminary in California; founder and international team leader of African Enterprise, which seeks to train others to evangelize the cities of Africa through word and deed in partnership with the church; evangelist, teacher, and ministry of reconciliation; his books include *Chasing the Wind* and *Bursting the Wineskins*. 342, 349, 369, 375

Catherwood, Sir Fred (1925–)—Sir Fred was born in Castledown, northern Ireland, and has been involved in business and public service with the UK government; he was elected to the European Parliament, has been president of the Evangelical Alliance since 1992, and vice president of the Interna-

tional Fellowship of Evangelical Students since 1991; his books include *A Better Way—the Case for a Christian Social Order*. 367

Chalke, Rev. Steve (1955–)—Steve comes from Croydon, and is the founding director of the Oasis Trust, which he set up to make Christianity relevant via social action, training, and resourcing the church; a regular broadcaster on television and radio, he is also author of many books, including *More Than Meets the Eye*. 362

Chambers, Oswald (1874–1917)—Preacher, teacher, and writer; his many books are the result of his wife's shorthand notes of his lectures and addresses; he died while working with the YMCA among troops in Egypt. 68, 110, 145, 228, 279, 315, 332

Clement of Alexandria (c.150–c.220)—Born into a pagan family, but thirsted for truth; argued that the Christian truth was a superior form of philosophy while rejecting agnosticism; became head of the catechetical school of Alexandria. 135

Clement of Rome, St. (d. c. 101)—Believed to be the fourth bishop of Rome; his letter of rebuke to Christians at Corinth over immorality established some authority at Rome; possibly martyred under Domitian. 152

Collyer, Robert (1813–1912)—Born in Yorkshire, Robert worked in the local mill as a child and became the town blacksmith in Ilkley; he emigrated to the United States in 1850, was involved in the U.S. Sanitary Commission, and pastored churches in Chicago and New York. 234, 300, 308, 361

Confederate Soldier—Attributed to an unnamed soldier just before the final battle of Richmond in which he died. Prayer submitted by Senator Max Cleland (D-GA). 59

Cowper, William (1731–1800)—
Born in Berkhampstead, Hertfordshire; for most of his life he suffered
bouts of acute suicidal depression;
John Newton had Cowper (pro-
nounced "Cooper") to live and
help in parish work at Olney for
nineteen years; wrote poems and
sixty-eight hymns which were published with those of the Newtons
in the *Olney Collection*—including
"There Is a Fountain Filled With
Blood" and "God Moves in a Mys-
terious Way." 168

Cranmer, Archbishop Thomas
(1489–1556)—Favored by Henry
VIII after giving him matrimonial
advice, and then promoted to archbishop of Canterbury, introduced
Reformation ideas into Anglican
worship and practice; compiled the
Book of Common Prayer in 1549;
sentenced for high treason under
Queen Mary and burned at the
stake with Nicholas Ridley, his
chaplain. 44, 134, 242, 292, 299,
322

Crosby, Frances Jane "Fanny" (1810–
1915)—Though blind, she taught
English and history at the New
York Institute for the blind and
wrote over nine thousand hymns,
including "Blessed Assurance" and
"To God Be the Glory"; dedicated
her life to serving the poorest and
neediest—most of her income from
writing went toward this work. 259

Cyril of Alexandria, St. (c. 376–
444)—Born in Alexandria, Egypt;
considered the most outstanding
theologian of Alexandria; known
especially for his work on the doctrines of the Trinity and the Person
of Christ; stood against the heresies
of Nestorius. 280

Dawson, George (1811–1876)—Pastor of a small Baptist chapel at
Rickmansworth before shooting to
fame as minister of the Church of
the Savior, an independent church

in Birmingham; internationally
famous for his lectures; though not
considered bound by any creed, his
prayers demonstrate a devout and
reverent mind. 61, 143, 199, 249,
257, 298

Dearmer, Jessie Mabel (d. 1915)—First
wife of the Rev. Percy Dearmer;
died while serving with her husband in Serbia. 93

Dearmer, Rev. Percy (1867–1936)—
Percy was born in London; he ministered at Primrose Hill up to the
First World War, when he and his
wife, Mabel, served with the British Red Cross in Serbia; later work
included the YMCA in France,
Mission of Help, India, and canon
of Westminster Abbey; authority
on worship and writer of hymns,
including "He Who Would Val-
iant Be." 356

Dekker, Thomas (1570–1631)—Play-
wright during the reign of James
I; *Prayer for a Soldier* was possibly
republished by him; having been
written originally by someone else.
262

Dimitri of Rastov, St. (1651–1709)—
Russian bishop; celebrated as a
preacher and writer. 182

Dobson, Dr. James (1936–)—Dr.
Dobson was born in Louisiana
and is founder and president of
Focus on the Family, an evangelical
organization devoted to the pres-
ervation of the home and spread of
the gospel; widely recognized as a
leading authority on today's family;
he is also an author and television
presenter, his books include *When
God Doesn't Make Sense*, *Straight
Talk to Men*, and *Parenting Isn't for
Cowards*. 119

Drake, Sir Francis (c. 1539–1596)—
Born in Devon, he received an
appointment "among the seamen
in the king's navy to read prayers to
them" and was ordained a deacon,
taking holy orders based near Cha-

tham; he then became a privateer, the first Englishman to circumnavigate the globe and, as Elizabeth's vice-admiral, he defeated the Spanish Armada. 38

Dudley-Smith, Rt. Rev. Timothy (1926–)—Born in Manchester, he has been an Anglican minister in Erith, Bermondsey, and Norwich, and Bishop of Thetford; editorial secretary of the Evangelical Alliance and editor of *Crusade Magazine*; author and hymn writer, whose hymns include "Tell Out My Soul the Greatness of the Lord." Some of the prayers listed here have been abbreviated with the author's permission. 13, 85, 219, 240, 301

Dye, Rev. Colin (1953–)—Colin was born in Kenya and is senior minister of Kensington Temple and leader of the London City Church, one of the largest in the UK; he has a passion for reaching the lost and seeing them discipled into a strong and lasting faith. 167

Eareckson Tada, Joni (1949–)—Joni was born in Baltimore, Maryland; paralyzed by a diving accident in 1967. She is now a writer, singer, and convention speaker. She is known worldwide for her work among children and adults, inspiring millions to trust in God and His sovereignty. 115

Edwards, Rev. Joel (1951–)—Joel was born in Jamaica and was appointed general director of the Evangelical Alliance in 1997. Previously he had been a probation officer and general secretary of the African and Caribbean Evangelical Alliance. He is an ordained minister of the New Testament Church of God and is married with two children. 256

Ellis, Rufus J. (1819–1885)—Missionary to Bengal; wrote a manual of Christian duty called *The Light of Life.* 222

Ephrem the Syrian, St. (c. 306–373)—

Christian poet who wrote over one thousand works involving over three million lines; defended the faith against gnosticism and Arians; died while ministering to plague victims. 207

Erasmus, Desiderius (1467–1536)—Although he was Dutch, Erasmus was based in Basel, Switzerland; compiled the first edition of the New Testament in Greek with a Latin translation and notes (which were affixed to the reading desk in many parish churches by royal edict); sympathetic to the Reformation; described by Luther as "our future and our hope"; never separated from Rome, though it was said that "Erasmus laid the egg and Luther hatched it." 89, 147, 170, 183, 253, 280

Everard, George (nineteenth century)—Vicar in Dover, Southport, and Wolverhampton; wrote several devotional books and compilations. 82

Fénelon, François de Salignac de la Mothe (1651–1715)—French bishop, respected for his learning and piety; critical of the coercion of Huguenot converts. 35

Fisher, Julia (1952–)—Born in London, Julia is a writer and broadcaster. She is currently a presenter and features editor with London's Premier Radio. 347

Forster, Roger (1933–)—Roger was born in London and became the founder and leader of the Ichthus Christian Fellowship and cofounder of March for Jesus. He is also vice-president of the Evangelical Alliance and of Tearfund. His interest in students is reflected in his one-time vice-presidency of the University and Colleges Christian Fellowship. 211

Francis of Assisi, St. (c. 1181–1226)—After a career as a soldier, he established the Franciscan order.

He was committed to alleviating poverty, and he initially ministered to leprosy victims. He preached a spiritual rather than a physical crusade after being disillusioned by the behavior of the Crusaders. 118, 217

Fuller, Thomas (1608–1661)—English clergyman and writer; chaplain to Charles II, best known for his *History of the Worthies of Britain*. 139

Gelasian Sacramentary (c. 490)—Compiled by Gelasius, bishop of Rome, who composed many prayers and revised many that were already in use. 30, 183, 198, 387, 295, 342, 364

Graham, Billy (1918–)—A Baptist preacher who had developed a worldwide ministry by the 1950s through mass crusades in various stadiums and major convention halls. Books, magazines, radio, and television established him as an international figure. He is also a confidant of film stars and American presidents. He is thought to have preached to more people than any other evangelist. 12

Greek Liturgy—Liturgy of the Greek Orthodox Church, originating from the third century. 87

Gregory of Nazianzus, St. (c. 329–c.390)—Theologian and doctor of the church; known for his work on Origen's works and also as bishop of Constantinople; preferred an ascetic, monastic life to public life. X254XX

Grey, Lady Jane (1537–1554)—Great granddaughter of Henry VII; queen of England for nine days, but forced to abdicate in favor of Mary Tudor and was then imprisoned in the Tower of London; beheaded with her husband, Lord Dudley. 150

Guyon, Madame Jeanne Marie-de-la-Mothe (1648–1717)—French mystic and writer; born in Montargis, France; wanted to become a nun but was instead married unhappily at sixteen and widowed at twenty-eight; devoted her life to the poor and needy and to piety, and became the center for the pious movement known as Quietism; imprisoned in the Bastille for her beliefs. 240

Hacking, Rev. Philip (1931–)—Born in Blackburn; Anglican minister in Edinburgh and Sheffield. He was chairman of the Keswick Convention 1984–1993 and is currently chairman of Reform and Word Alive. 365

Haggai, John Edmund (1924–)—Founder of the Haggai Institute, a unique provider of advanced leadership training to leaders in over 150 developing nations. His vision for world evangelism has taken him around the globe more than 80 times. 330

Hall, Thomas (1610–1665)—Born in Worcester, he became a nonconformist pastor and writer based at King's Norton. 63, 71, 169, 250, 314

Hammarskjöld, Dag H. A. C. (1905–1961)—Born in Jonköping, Sweden. He served as chairman of the Bank of Sweden, Swedish foreign minister and, in 1953, secretary general of the United Nations—a role he described as "the curator of the secrets of eighty-two nations." During this time he was especially involved in peace negotiations in the Middle East and the Congo. 225

Hare, Maria (1798–1870)—Wife of an Anglican clergyman at Alton and, after widowhood in 1834, based at Herstmonceux, Sussex; letter writer and devout Christian. 281

Havergal, Frances Ridley (1836–1879)—Born in Astley, Worcestershire, a child of the rectory; scholar, poet, and hymn writer, whose

hymns include, "Lord, Speak to Me That I May Speak," "Take My Life and Let It Be," and "I Gave My Life for Thee." 295

Henry, Matthew (1662–1714)—Born in Shropshire, and became a Presbyterian pastor in nearby Chester. Preacher, writer, and biblical commentator, he is best known for his magnum opus: *Exposition of the Old and New Testament*. 24, 103, 171, 220, 260, 337, 374

Henry, Dr. Carl F. H. (1913–) Theologian, author, editor, and lecturer. Carl was born in New York City and became a newspaper reporter and editor before becoming a Christian and turning to theology. He served at the Eastern Baptist, Northern Baptist, and Fuller Theological seminaries. He is the founding editor of *Christianity Today* and author of more than forty books including the six-volume work *God, Revelation and Authority*. 176, 245

Henry VI (1411–1471)—Born in Windsor, son of Henry V; became king in 1422 as an infant; known as the "Royal Saint" due to his piety. However, his inability to govern led to the War of the Roses. In 1461 he was deposed and exiled. He was restored briefly but later murdered in the Tower of London; founder of Eton and King's College, Cambridge. 143

Higham, Rev. W. Vernon (1916–)—Vernon was born in Caernarfon, Wales, and left teaching to become a pastor in the Presbyterian Church of Wales. He ministered in a mining town and in the mountains and has been pastor of Heath Evangelical Church, Cardiff, since 1962. The hymns he has written include "There Is a Rock on Which I Stand" and "Great Is the Gospel of Our Glorious God." 223

How, Rt. Rev. William Walsham (1823–1897)—Born at Shrews-bury and entered the Anglican ministry, ministering at Kidderminster, Shrewsbury, Whittington, and London. He later became bishop of East London, where he was loved for his work among the poor, and bishop of Wakefield. An author and hymn writer, his hymns include "For All the Saints" and "O Word of God Incarnate." 48

Howard-Browne, Rodney (1961–)—Senior pastor of The River, Tampa, Florida; known also as the father of the "Toronto Blessing." Born in South Africa, Rodney and his family moved to America in the 1980s to engage in an itinerant ministry. The Holy Spirit fell on a small congregation near Albany, New York, largely through the ministry of the laying on of hands. This eventually spread to Canada and then all over the world. 7

Hudson Taylor, James (1832–1905)—Born in Barnsley, James became a missionary in China and founded the China Inland Mission (CIM), later known as the Overseas Missionary Fellowship (OMF), the largest Christian missionary organization in China and the precursor of "faith missions." 278, 316

Hughes, Rev. Selwyn (1928–)—Born in Glamorgan, Wales; founder and director of Crusade for World Revival (CWR), which is dedicated to encouraging prayer for revival and daily Bible reading; author for over thirty years of the daily reading notes *Every Day With Jesus*; developed CWR's counselor training program internationally. 32, 133, 187, 312

Hume, Cardinal George Basil (1913–1999)—Born in Newcastle-upon-Tyne; trained as an English Benedictine monk and became abbot of Ampleforth in 1963, then the Roman Catholic Archbishop of Westminster in 1976. 58, 208

Hunter, John (1849–1917)—Trained at Mansfield College, Oxford, he became Congregational minister of the King's Weigh House, London; preacher and writer. 98

Ibaim, Akanu—Nigerian Christian. 189

Ignatius of Loyola, St. (1491–1556)—Spanish soldier; while wounded he read the life of Christ and was inspired to an intense life of discipleship; became a religious leader, founding the Society of Jesus (Jesuits); sent missionaries to Japan, India, and Brazil; founded schools for children; opposed the Reformation. 60

Ioannikos, St. (c. 752–846)—Greek ascetic. Following a career as a soldier, Ioannikos became a monk at Mount Olympus in Bythinia (Asia Minor/Turkey). He was an opponent of the Iconoclasts. 42

Jack, Victor (1937–)—Victor was born in Saxmundham, Suffolk, and has been an evangelist with Counties' Evangelistic Work and director of Sizewell Hall Christian Conference Centre. In 2000 he became the chairman of the Garden Tomb Association, Jerusalem, and the occasional chaplain to the tomb. 278, 316

James, Walter (1879–1908)—Born in Portsmouth. A Wesleyan Methodist minister, James died after only fifteen months in the ministry. An original, vigorous and picturesque preacher, much acclaimed by all. He pastored in Lewisham, Kensington, and Surrey. 49, 76, 128, 172, 276, 325, 343

Jenks, Rev. Benjamin (1646–1724)—Rector of Harley, Shropshire, and chaplain to Earl of Bradford; he wrote a popular family devotional book. 213, 285

John, J. (1958–)—J. John comes from London, is a speaker and writer, and is married to Killy. They have three sons. J. John says, "I love Jesus and enjoy life, leisure, food, and movies." 291

Jones, Rt. Rev. James (1948–)—James was born in Glasgow and became a teacher and cofounder of the first Volunteer Bureau in England. He jointed Scripture Union, in audiovisuals, before entering the Anglican ministry. He has served in Bristol and Croydon. He was bishop of Hull and, since 1998, has been bishop of Liverpool. A writer and broadcaster, he is married to Sarah and has three teenage daughters. 273, 377

Jowett, Rev. John H. (1863–1923)—Known in his day as "the greatest preacher in the English-speaking world." Born in Yorkshire, he entered the Congregational ministry and ministered at Carrs Lane, Birmingham (after R. W. Dale), New York, and then at Westminster Chapel, London. His writings include God Our Contemporary and The School of Calvary. 33, 65, 227, 285

Kempis, Thomas à (c. 1379–1471)—Born in Kempen, Prussia, he entered the monastery of Mount Saint Agnes where he spent most of his life copying manuscripts and giving counsel. He is author of Imitation of Christ, a devotional treatise. 31, 90, 157, 194, 266, 296, 340, 354

Ken, Thomas (1637–1711)—Born in Little Berkhampstead, Hertfordshire, he was bishop of Bath and Wells and also a hymn writer; his hymns include "Awake My Soul," "Glory to Thee My God This Night," and the doxology "Praise God From Whom All Blessings Flow"; he refused to take the oath of allegiance to William of Orange in 1688. 53, 152, 372

Kendrick, Graham (1950–)—Comes from Northamptonshire and is a well-known worship leader and composer; his songs and hymns are sung around the world and include "Shine, Jesus, Shine." 286

Kennedy, Dr. D. James (1930–)—Dr. Kennedy was born in Augusta, Georgia, is senior minister of Coral Ridge Presbyterian Church, Fort Lauderdale, Florida, and the founding president of Evangelism Explosion International; chancellor of Knox Theological Seminary; television and radio broadcaster. 75, 197

Lacey, Graham Ferguson (1948–)— Graham comes from Solihull. He is an entrepreneur and lay preacher involved in several inspirational worldwide projects. He was the principal mover behind "The Millennium Chorus," Graham Kendrick's work for the Millennium. Graham lives with his wife, Susan, and their sons, Luke and James, in the Isle of Man. 344

Larcombe, Jennifer Rees (1942–)— Jennifer was born in London, spent eight years in a wheelchair while her six children were still small, and received wonderful healing through prayer in 1990. She has written twenty-two books, including *Beyond Healing*. She works for the organization Beauty From Ashes, whose aim is to help those suffering from trauma and loss. 18, 100, 153, 265

Lawrence, Brother (seventeenth century)—Born in France, he was converted at the age of eighteen and later became a monk with the order of the "Discalced Carmelites." He is best known as the author of *The Practice of the Presence of God* in which he sets out his spiritual principles: an overwhelming delight in God and the practice of deep submission to God. His real name is Nicolas Herman. 79, 224

Liturgy of Geneva (first printed c. 1542)—Originally adapted from Martin Bucer's German by Calvin. 146, 329, 341

Liturgy of St. Mark—Used at Alexandria and named after St. Mark; now generally assigned to the fourth century or later. 95

Liturgy of Syrian Jacobites (third century)—Liturgy of the Syrian Jacobite Church. All Syrian Jacobite liturgies are thought to be derived from St. James; "James" being "Jacob" in Greek. 177

Lloyd-Jones, Dr. D. Martyn (1899–1981)—A Welshman with a brilliant medical career ahead of him, he answered God's call to the ministry in 1923 as pastor in the Welsh Calvinistic Methodist Church. Characterized by a remarkable openness to the Holy Spirit, he has been described as the greatest theologian-preacher since the Puritan John Owen. He served as a minister at Westminster Chapel between 1939 and 1968, initially as Campbell Morgan's associate, and rapidly became the natural choice as minister to students. His expository sermons—for example, "The Sermon on the Mount, Romans and Ephesians"—are still being published. 72, 186, 366, 371

Longfellow, Henry Wadsworth (1807–1882)—Born in Portland, Maine, in the United States; professor of modern languages and literature at Harvard; best known today for his poems "The Wreck of the Hesperus," "The Village Blacksmith," "Evangeline," and "The Tale of Hiawatha." 67

Lunn, Rev. Sir Henry S. (1859–1939)—Born into an old Lincolnshire Methodist family; entered the Wesleyan Methodist ministry in 1882 and spent a year in India before his time there was curtailed by ill health. The controversies he raised regarding missionary policies in India led to his resignation from the ministry. He organized ecumenical conferences in Switzerland which led to the foundation of the Lunn travel company; joined the Anglican church in 1910; wrote *The Love of Jesus*, a manual of prayer, meditation, and preparation for Holy Communion, in 1911. 109, 145

Luther, Martin (1485–1546)—German reformer. As professor of biblical exegesis at Wittenberg, he opposed corrupt practices of the church and preached the doctrine of salvation by faith alone. Nailing his ninety-five theses to the Wittenberg church door, he started the fire of the Reformation. "He possessed the power of kindling other souls with the fire of his own convictions." 136, 235

Lutheran Service Book—Prayers and orders of worship for Lutheran churches. 221

Marshall, Peter (1902–1949)—Born in Coatbridge, Scotland, Peter served in the British Navy but sensed a call to the ministry. He graduated from Columbia Theological Seminary, Georgia, was pastor of New York Avenue Presbyterian Church, Washington DC, and, in 1948, became chaplain to the U.S. Senate. He wrote *Mr. Jones* and *Meet the Master* and was the subject of the book and film titled *A Man Called Peter*. 21, 139

Martin, Samuel (1817–1878)—Born and raised in Woolwich, south London, Martin became the first minister of Westminster Chapel at the age of twenty-five. He was not only widely respected for his preaching, but he also had a great concern for both the young and the poor of the Westminster slums, and inspired his congregation to be involved in caring for the poor. He

was a friend of Lord Shaftesbury. 114, 239, 321

Matheson, Rev. George (1842–1906)—Church of Scotland minister in Edinburgh; almost totally blind, but was an academically gifted church historian and theologian; able to memorize sermons and entire sections of the Bible. Listeners were often unaware that he was blind. He wrote hymns, including "O Love That Wilt Not Let Me Go" and "Make Me a Captive, Lord." 112, 192

McNee, Sir David (1925–)—David was born in Glasgow into a Christian home and has always had involvement in the Scottish evangelistic movements, including Tell Scotland; and served as chairman during Billy Graham's mission in 1991; joined the police force in Glasgow in 1946 after war-time service in the Royal Navy, becoming chief constable of Glasgow and then Strathclyde, and finally commissioner of police of the Metropolis (London). 326

Melancthon, Philip (Schwarzerd) (1497–1560)—German Protestant reformer, associate and fellow worker with Luther; composed the Augsburg Confession (1530); led the Reformation movement after Luther's death; wrote *Loci Communes* in 1521—the first great Protestant work on dogmatic theology. 36, 121, 188

Methodist Book of Offices—1936 orders of service for the Methodist church, which draws on Christian devotion through the ages. 80

Morgan, Dr. G. Campbell (1863–1945)—Campbell was born in the afterglow of the 1859 Revival, and by his early twenties had an international preaching ministry. In the United States he was seen as D. L. Moody's successor. In London, where he was minister of Westminster Chapel (1904–1917 and 1935–1943), he was spoken of as successor to Spurgeon. His books are still popular, especially in the United States. 368

Motyer, Rev. Alec (1924–)—Born in Dublin, Alec first sensed a call to the ministry at the age of six, though he was not converted until he was fifteen. He has ministered in Wolverhampton, Bristol, London, and Bournemouth, before teaching Hebrew and Old Testament at Clifton, Tyndale Hall, and Trinity colleges in Bristol. He is a writer, convention speaker, and specialist on Isaiah. 274, 302

Mozarabic Liturgy—The ancient liturgy of Spain until the eleventh century. 71, 231

Murray, Andrew (1828–1917)—South African religious leader and writer; ordained into the Dutch Reformed church, he became an itinerant evangelistic preacher after revival broke out in his parish. He placed an emphasis on prayer and personal holiness, and wrote With Christ in the School of Prayer in 1885. Also concerned for the welfare of Africans, he opposed Afrikaner nationalism and British colonialism. 160

Nestorian Liturgy—Named after Nestorius (d. 451), a zealous ascetic. Nestorians are concentrated in Kurdistan, Iraq and (a few) in India. 73

Newman, John Henry (1801–1890)—Born in London, he became a preacher and founder of the Tractarian movement; became a Roman Catholic priest in 1845 and established the Birmingham Oratory; appointed cardinal; wrote the hymn "Lead Kindly Light" and "Dream of Gerontius"—the latter was set to music by Elgar. 15, 102, 181, 255, 307, 345, 358

Origen (c. 185–255) Born in Alexandria and became head of the Catechetical school there at the age of eighteen. A preacher and teacher, he opened a school at Caesarea, but suffered during persecution under Decius. The first systematic theologian, Origen sought to establish a reliable text of the Old Testament, and is known especially for his On First Principles. 54, 164

Orthodox Way Christmas Day Vespers, The—A book about the Greek Orthodox church, its doctrines, discipline, and devotional life; written by Bishop Kallistes Ware. 370

Ould, Rev. Fielding (d. 1864)—The vicar of Christ Church, Hunter Street, Liverpool, he is especially known for Trinitarian teaching. 78

Palau, Luis (1934–)—Luis was born in Buenos Aires, Argentina. He committed his life to Christ at the age of twelve, started preaching at eighteen, and had a tent and radio ministry by his twenties. The Luis Palau Evangelistic Team has an international preaching ministry—thirteen million in sixty-eight nations to date, and even wider radio and television ministry. He is also a prolific writer, whose books include Where Is God When Bad Things Happen? 278

Parsons, Dianne (1949–)—Born in Cardiff, Wales, and married to Rob, Dianne works with Care for the Family and is the presenter of The Issues Women Face seminar series. 346

Parsons, Rob (1948–)—Rob was born in Cardiff, Wales, and is executive director of Care for the Family. He is the author of a number of books including The Sixty-Minute Father, The Sixty-Minute Marriage, and The Sixty-Minute Mother. 351

Pascal, Blaise (1613–1662)—Born in Clermont-Ferrand, France; French mathematician, physicist, theologian, and philosopher. His experiments with mercury led to the invention of the barometer, hydraulic press, and syringe. He patented a calculating machine, and his studies led to the invention of integral calculus. His *Pensées* (*Thoughts*) show profound thought on Christian truth. 107

Patrick, St. (c. 385–c. 461)—Born in Scotland of Roman Catholic parents, but kidnapped and sold into slavery in Ireland. His experiences led him to spiritual discovery, and he became a missionary. Appointed bishop to Ireland, he preached to thousands, mainly in the spiritually barren areas in the north and west, establishing communes. He wrote *Epistola* in which he contemplated the ill treatment of Irish Christians by the British. 88

Patrick, Bishop Symon (1626–1707)— Bishop of Ely. 160

Perry, Rt. Rev. John (1935–)—John was born in Mill Hill, London, and has been vicar at St. Andrew's, Chorleywood, warden of Lee Abbey, bishop of Southampton and, since 1996, bishop of Chelmsford. He is author of *Effective Christian Leadership* and has a wide involvement in the Christian healing ministry. 205

Philaret (1553–1633)—Metropolitan bishop of Moscow. 29

Polycarp (c.70–c.155)—Possibly a disciple of St. John; bishop of Smyrna (modern Izmir); especially known for his martyrdom. When invited to recant, he replied, "Eighty-six years I have served Him, and He has done me no wrong; how then can I blaspheme my King who saved me?" 206

Prayers for Social and Family Worship—Prayers prepared by the Church of Scotland in 1862. 117, 138, 214, 252, 329

Prime, Rev. Derek (1931–)—Derek was born in London and has served as pastor in Lansdowne Evangelical Free Church, London, and in Charlotte Chapel, Edinburgh. Since 1987 he has devoted his time to writing and an itinerant ministry. 74, 131, 178, 323, 352

Procter, Adelaide Anne (1825–1864)— (Pseudonym: Mary Berwick) English poet, born in London; contributed to Dickens's *Household Words*; her poems include "The Lost Chord," set to music by Sir Arthur Sullivan. 215

Pusey, Edward B. (1800–1882)—English theologian and leader of the Oxford movement; born in Pusey, Berkshire; religious professor of Hebrew at Oxford; translated Augustine's *Confessions* and the works of Tertullian; built churches in east London and Leeds. 16, 70, 124, 177, 238, 272, 328

Rauschenbusch, Walter (1861–1918)— Born in Rochester, New York; an American clergyman; professor at Rochester Theological Seminary; leader of the Social Gospel movement, stressing social issues as being one of the purposes of Christianity. 190

Redpath, Alan (1907–1989)—Left a successful career in business at God's call to be an evangelist and Bible teacher with National Young Life Campaign; became pastor of Duke St. Baptist Church, Moody Memorial Church, Chicago, and Charlotte Baptist Chapel, Edinburgh; was widely known as a conference speaker and writer. 205

Rees, Tom (1911–1970)—International Bible teacher and evangelist, writer and broadcaster; conducted United Church campaigns and organized camps for boys from the slums; emphasis on reaching university students; filled Royal Albert Hall over fifty times; committed most of the Bible to memory. 236

Reynolds, Bishop Edward (1599–1676)—Bishop of Norwich, remembered for moderate treatment of dissenters; involved in Savoy Conference, 1661; Wesley included some of Reynold's sermons in his Christian library for his preachers. 39

Richard de Wyche of Chichester (c.1197–1253)—Born in Droitwich, son of a yeoman farmer; chancellor of Oxford and chancellor to the archbishop of Canterbury; regarded as a model diocesan bishop—charitable and accessible, generous to the poor during times of famine. 45

Ridley, Nicholas (c.1500–1555)—Born near Haltwhistle, Northumberland. His various posts included chaplain to Thomas Cranmer and Henry VIII, bishop of Rochester and bishop of London. He helped Cranmer prepare the Thirty-nine Articles of the Church of England. On the death of Edward VI, he denounced Mary I and Elizabeth I as illegitimate and espoused the cause of Lady Jane Grey, but was executed when Mary became queen. 111

Roman Breviary—The book of prayer for the Roman Catholic Church, compiled over many centuries; in its full form it runs to several volumes, and was originally published in Latin. 217

Rossetti, Christina (1830–1894)—English poet; born in London, the sister of Dante G. Rossetti. Her hymns include "Love Came Down at Christmas" and "In the Bleak Mid-Winter." 38, 55, 61, 105, 126, 182

Rowlandson, Maurice (1925–) Born in London, Maurice was called to "full-time" Christian work at Keswick. He trained in Minnesota when Billy Graham was president of his college and has worked with him since. Secretary of the Keswick Convention, magistrate, lieutenant commander in the Royal Navy Reserve; author; founder and president of the Venturers' Norfolk Broads Cruise for Youngsters. 148, 297

Russell, George (1935–) George comes from Edinburgh and is in business in the private and public sectors. He is actively engaged in Christian interests such as CARE, Mission Scotland, and Allander Evangelical Church, Milngavie. He lives in Glasgow with his wife, Moira. They have three children and two grandchildren. 184, 306

Sangster, Rev. Dr. William Edwin (1900–1960)—Methodist minister renowned as an evangelist, preacher, and writer. He ministered at Scarborough, Leeds, and Westminster Central Hall where he served Londoners through the Blitz by visiting the shelters. Twice he was president of the Methodist Conference. He was known nationally for a sermon he gave in 1952, entitled "A Sermon to Britain," about the moral condition of the land. He was convinced of the need for revival. 254

Scripture Union Prayers for Schools, Youth Groups, Church Services, and Personal Use—A collection of prayers compiled by Godfrey Robinson and Stephen Winward and published in 1967. 33, 46, 51, 203, 253, 283, 331

Serapion (d. c. 550)—Bishop of Thmuis (or Thumis) in the Egyptian delta; a contemporary of St. Athanasius and St. Anthony. 69, 168

Shaftesbury, Lord (1801–1885)—Seventh earl of Shaftesbury, also known as Lord Ashley; English reformer and philanthropist, involved in factory, housing, army schools, and mines reform. 37

Slater, Richard (1854–1939)—Father of Salvation Army music, a "pioneering giant" of the Salvation Army; also a prolific songwriter, writing the lyrics and/or music of a total of 851 songs—587 of them published during his lifetime; served at Regent Hall, Hoxton, Tottenham, New Barnet, and Wood Green. 66

Spurgeon, Charles H. (1834–1892)—English Baptist preacher; born in Kelvedon, Essex; pastored at the Metropolitan Tabernacle, seating six thousand; emphasis on the evangelical nature of the Baptist Union, which led to his separation from it in 1887; prolific writer; he established a training college for young preachers and an orphanage. 27, 101, 141, 179, 218, 243, 284, 290, 333, 376

Stevenson, Robert Louis (1850–1894)—Scottish writer born in Edinburgh; afflicted by constant illnesses, including tuberculosis; famous for his books: *Treasure Island, Kidnapped, Catriona,* and *The Strange Case of Dr. Jekyll and Mr. Hyde*; also wrote a book of prayers while travelling in Samoa. 130, 193, 338, 354

Stobart, Rev. Henry (c. 1820–1890)—Graduating from Oxford in 1847, Henry served in the Church of England from 1849 to the 1880s and was rector of Warkton near Kettering 1865–1881; author of *Daily Services for Christian Households.* 354

Stott, Dr. John (1921–)—John was born in London; was rector of All Souls Church, Langham Place, London from 1950 to 1975, and is now rector emeritus there; he has written a number of books, including *Basic Christianity*; he was appointed honorary chaplain to the queen in 1959. 23, 65, 283

Stowe, Harriet (Elizabeth) Beecher (1811–1896)—American novelist, born in Litchfield, Connecticut; raised in a puritanical family and married a theologian; famous for *Uncle Tom's Cabin,* published in 1852. 28

Sursum Corda—Latin for "Lift Up Your Hands." Four-line exhortation as part of the liturgy at the start of prayer. From the Anaphora of St. Mark, a primitive liturgy from the second century. 305, 339

Symeon, St. (949–1022)—Known as the New Theologian; Byzantine monk and mystic. Prayer was very important in St. Symeon's life. He was abbot of St. Mamas monastery, but the monks rebelled against his austere regime; he put emphasis on individual experience and believed that all Christians are capable of knowing God directly through prayer. 81, 163

Synesius of Cyrene (B.C. 375)—Pagan intellectual who became a Christian in order to serve the Christian society of his day; strenuous defender of his flock. 113

Taylor, Jeremy (1613–1667)—English theologian, born in Cambridge; chaplain to Archbishop Laud; imprisoned during the Civil War; became vice chancellor of Dublin University and a member of the Irish Privy Council; his writings are considered to be among the most eloquent sacred writings in the English language. 40, 144, 251, 303

ten Boom, Corrie (1892–1983)—Dutch evangelist and author; helped seven hundred Jews escape during the Second World War, which led to her imprisonment in 1944. Following her unexpected release from Ravensbrück, she established a rehabilitation home for concentration camp victims in Holland and a home for refugees in Germany. Her books include *The*

Hiding Place and *Tramp for the Lord.* 34, 73, 77, 113, 194, 206, 225, 252, 259, 284, 297, 353

Teresa of Calcutta, Mother (1910–1997)—Born in Yugoslavia of Albanian parents. She became principal of a convent school in India but left the convent to work in the slums of Calcutta. She opened a Home for the Dying in 1952 and founded the Order of Missionaries of Charity, which is now at work in two hundred houses in several countries. 363

Teresa of Avila, St. (1515–1582)—Born in Avila and sent to a convent at sixteen. She became ill and partially paralyzed for several years but saw visions of Christ, which strengthened her spiritual life. She founded thirty communities for women and for men. 262

Tersteegen, Gerhard (1697–1769)—Born in Mews, Prussia; German preacher and prolific hymn writer; experienced revival in his church at Mulheim in 1751; his hymns include "Lo, God Is Here!," "Let Us Adore," and "God Reveals His Presence." 304, 364

Thornhill, Rev. Alan F. (1908–)—Chaplain of Hertford College, Oxford. 271

Thornton, Henry (1760–1815)—Member of Parliament, philanthropist and economist; influential member of Clapham Sect alongside Wilberforce; supported anti-slavery campaign, and was also involved in the Church Missionary Society, and the British and Foreign Bible Society; gave away over 80 per cent of his income; he has several publications to his name, including a book of family prayers. 132, 161, 231

Tileston, Mary (d. 1895)—Compiled devotional books. 64, 87

Toplady, Augustus Montague (1740–1778)—English Calvinist clergyman and hymn writer; born in Farnham, Surrey; vicar of Broadhembury in Devon, and preacher in the Orange Street Calvinistic Methodist chapel near Leicester Fields, London. His hymns include "A Debtor to Mercy Alone" and "Rock of Ages." 55, 106, 196, 310, 319

Torrance, Professor Thomas F. (1913–)—Born in China of missionary parents, Professor Torrance lectured in church history and Christian dogmatics at Edinburgh University; especially concerned to root students in Reformed dogmatics and to introduce interest in the Greek Orthodox Church; moderator of the General Assembly of the Church of Scotland; awarded the Templeton prize. 36, 77, 251, 302, 357

Tutu, Desmond Mpilo (1931–)—Desmond was born in Klerksdorp in North-West Province, ordained an Anglican priest in 1960 and has been dean of Johannesburg, bishop of Lesotho, and the first black general secretary of the South African Council of Churches; awarded the Nobel Peace Prize in recognition of "the courage and heroism shown by black South Africans in their use of peaceful methods in the struggle against apartheid." 17, 19, 129, 247

Washington, George (1732–1799)—Born in Virginia, he was the richest man in the land; rose through the ranks of the British army in the Colonies and defeated the British forces with the aid of France in 1781. He retired from the army to form a government. He drew up the American Constitution and became the first president of the United States. 64

Weatherhead, Dr. Leslie (1893–1976)—Methodist minister at Manchester, Leeds, and London (City Temple); popular Christian writer and academic, with a special interest in psychology and the healing power of prayer and faith. Weatherhead spoke to men and women in their difficulties, and understood suffering having served in the army during the First World War. His books include *A Private House of Prayer*. 47, 51, 122, 299, 324

Wesley, John (1703–1791)—Born in Epworth, Lincolnshire, son of a rector. At Oxford he headed a pious group nicknamed "The Holy Club" or "Oxford Methodists." He discovered the failings of piety as a missionary to Georgia and experienced the assurance of salvation by faith in a Moravian meeting in 1738. He traveled 250,000 miles on horseback, preaching 40,000 sermons. Though he sought to be loyal to the Church of England, Wesley was forced to break and form his own societies that later became known as the Methodist church. 62, 209, 255

Weston, Rev. Canon Keith (1926–)—Keith was born in Croydon, Surrey, and ministered in St. Ebbe's Church, Oxford, and as honorary canon of Christ Church Cathedral, Oxford; has also been an international speaker and chairman of the Keswick Convention. He is married to Margaret and has four children and seven grandchildren. Though retired, Keith is still busy preaching. 287, 317, 359

Williams, Rowland (1817–1870)—Tutor at King's College, Cambridge, and Professor of Hebrew at St. David's Theological College, Lampeter; known in his day for his studies on Christianity and Hinduism; contributor to the controversial *Essays and Reviews*; recognized for his integrity and search for the truth. 92, 267, 289, 327

Wimber, John (1954–1997)—John came from Peoria, Illinois, and was a professional jazz and pop musician. He received Christ in 1963 and became an evangelist and Bible teacher, placing an emphasis on evangelism and healing called "Power Evangelism." He was the founding director of church growth at the Fuller Institute of Evangelism, became leader of the Vineyard Christian Fellowship, and established an international ministry through writing and conferences. 21, 43

Yonggi Cho, Dr. David (1936–)—David was born in Kyungnam, Korea, and has become pastor of the world's largest church, Yoido Full Gospel Church, Seoul, which has more than 770,000 members. He is especially known for his teaching on the power of positive faith, prayer, principles of church growth, and home cell groups. 229

Youssef, Michael (1948–)—Michael Youssef is the founding pastor of the Church of the Apostles in Atlanta, Georgia. He is also the host and teacher on the Leading the Way radio and television ministries, heard daily on more than 600 stations in the United States and in more than 191 countries. 336

INDEX

POWERFUL *and* BALANCED
MESSAGES *of* TRUTH!

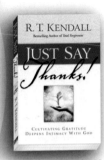

It's time to experience **THANKSGIVING** day daily!

Do you have a daily attitude of gratitude? *Just Say Thanks!* tackles a long-neglected and overlooked subject but one that is central to Christianity—thankfulness toward God and one another.

$13.99
1-59185-627-2
(Paperback)

True inner **PEACE** *awaits you!*

When everything in you wants to hold a grudge, point a finger, and remember the pain, God wants you to lay it all aside. *Total Forgiveness* will show you how to avoid spiritual quicksand and experience the incredible freedom found in total forgiveness.

$13.99
0-88419-889-8
(Paperback)

Understand why the **PAIN** just won't go away!

Do you want the prickly, uncomfortable thorn in your flesh to leave? *The Thorn in the Flesh* explains how God gives you thorns for your benefit. This book will help you realize that it is the best thing that will ever happen to you—next to your conversion and anointing.

$13.99
1-59185-612-4
(Paperback)

Call **800-599-5750** now, and mention offer #BP5402.
Or visit **www.charismahouse.com** to save **25%**!

5181

Strang Communications, the publisher of both Charisma House and *Charisma* magazine, wants to give you 3 FREE ISSUES of our award-winning magazine.

Since its inception in 1975, *Charisma* magazine has helped thousands of Christians stay connected with what God is doing worldwide.

Within its pages you will discover in-depth reports and the latest news from a Christian perspective, biblical health tips, global events in the body of Christ, personality profiles, and so much more. Join the family of *Charisma* readers who enjoy feeding their spirit each month with miracle-filled testimonies and inspiring articles that bring clarity, provoke prayer, and demand answers.

To claim your **3 free issues** of *Charisma,* send your name and address to: Charisma 3 Free Issue Offer, 600 Rinehart Road, Lake Mary, FL 32746. Or you may call 1-800-829-3346 and ask for Offer # 93FREE. This offer is only valid in the USA.

www.charismamag.com